CW00344905

WANTED ON VOYAGE

LD 4264720 7

Poetry is music written with words

WANTED ON VOYAGE

Wanda Barford

FlambardPress

First published in Great Britain in 2010 by Flambard Press
Holy Jesus Hospital, City Road, Newcastle upon Tyne NE1 2AS
www.flambardpress.co.uk

Typeset by BookType
Cover Design by Gainford Design Associates
Front cover painting: 'The Windsor Castle with a Tug, Final
Departure from Cape Town' (oil on canvas) by Harley Crossley
(Private Collection/The Bridgeman Art Library)
Printed in Great Britain by Bell & Bain, Glasgow, Scotland

A CIP catalogue record for this book is available from the British Library.

ISBN: 978-1-906601-18-8

Flambard Press wishes to thank Arts Council England
for its financial support.

Flambard Press is a member of Inpress.

The paper used for this book is FSC accredited.

for Naomi Lewis

who taught me so much

Acknowledgements

'Day of Atonement' and 'Shoes' first appeared in *Jewish Renaissance*; 'A POW to his Mother in Naples' received 3rd Prize in the Torriano Poetry Competition in 2006 and appeared in *Brittle Star* magazine; 'Standard Trading Company – Direct Importers' and 'Beauty and the Beast' were first published in *The Morley Review*; 'My Auntie Rica' was published in *Weyfarers*.

Also by Wanda Barford

Sweet Wine and Bitter Herbs
A Moon at the Door
Losing, Finding
What is the Purpose of Your Visit?

Contents

Three Union Castle Ships

1. *The Winchester Castle*

It's 1939 – I'm nine.
We're leaving Europe for Africa.
On board I feel seasick; father says
'go and ask the steward politely
if you can have an a-pple.'
I never get my apple but a chuckle instead.

Two English spinsters befriend me
and take photos of us three.
I'm on a ledge to appear taller;
we're all smiling.

2. *The Cape Town Castle*

'Croit encore à l'adieu suprême des mouchoirs'
  Stéphane Mallarmé

I run along the L-shaped mole
to the great ship anchored there,
eager to see those scenes again:
the long railing with the young girl waving,
waving her white hanky gravely;
and to smell the ozone of the sea,
the engines' oil, to touch the gangway's sticky handrail,
and feel the flat treads' ropey wobble under my feet.
But today I'm not allowed on board.

Looking down I see
the squarish stones that pave the pier –
they bring back how my stiletto heels
(yes, high fashion even then)
had stuck in the cracks several times,

as we, Vic, Renate, Tony and I,
disembarked to hit the town in search of
night-life, lights, excitement,
and the first fresh milk for weeks.

3. The Edinburgh Castle

Sarah, will you ever travel this way?
Night was the best. Inside they were dancing
the conga, the rumba, a slow-fox, then
a Paul Jones – I'll tell you some time what that is –
but outside on deck, that's where you want to be.
Alone, absolutely alone, watching the moon light up
the ship's wake while the parted waters rustle
with small splashing sounds, over and over again.

Then you'd want to look up and be dazzled
by this South Atlantic sky, where if you had a pin
you wouldn't find even a tiny space for it between the stars.

No, the stars wouldn't wink at you, they'd sing
a hundred tunes: canons, chorales, cantatas; sometimes
talk to you . . . but what they said I cannot tell.

Zimbabwean Drum at New End School, Hampstead

That African throb prompts me back,
it echoes a lion's roar,
its pulsating rhythm struck
by fingers and palm on a skin
stretched over the empty sound box,
evokes the veldt . . .

the heavy heat and long
nose-tickling grasses. I see
the sated lions – comatose after the kill –
licking their paws, yawning . . .
a heap of kudu bones beside them,
all in the shady circle of a msasa tree.

Nearby, those oven-hot rocks,
too burning for us to sit on at picnics,
the large ones perched on the small ones
so precariously we thought they'd slip off
while we gulped our ginger ale. But no,
they'd been like that for centuries.

And I see
the blinding sun baking the earth –
that red cracked earth
whose open-hand patterns
beg for rain . . .
Then a rumble of bare feet,

it's the dancers
with quivering hips and shaking
their ostrich-feathered head-gear
(skin blackened for the purpose).
They gyrate. But they're New End girls . . .
And alas! My dream fades.

Ghosts

*Zimbabwe National Park is the site of a ruined
town built, it is believed, by a Bantu people,
probably in the Middle Ages. The main ruins
are the elliptical 'Temple' and 'Acropolis', a
fortified citadel. The ruins were discovered in 1868.*

Who built that rounded tower?
Who placed the stones one
upon the other in a sunlit curve?

Slaves might have stood here
and here, lifting boulders, while
priests darkened the entrance

to the sanctum where veldt grasses
burned – the sound an antiphon
to their deep-throated chanting.

Passages encircle the inner circle,
crows perch by, ready to engorge
the blood of sacrificial beasts.

Timeless, soundless, the 'Acropolis'
stares down to where a granite frieze
graces the Temple Wall.

Then the rains begin,
washing clean the sacrificial blood,
the roofless houses, and the memory.

Standard Trading Company – Direct Importers, Proprietor: M. J. Simson

I remember your wholesaler's shop
with its two massive counters of teak
and the best silken rolls at the top
for the tall Shona girls who were chic.

With its two massive counters of teak
I'd awkwardly climb one and stay there.
I'd watch special buyers who were chic,
and you serving them with great care.

I'd climb up a counter and stay there
till you'd call me to move khaki drill
that didn't need nearly such care
as the carefully rolled satin twill.

You'd call me to move khaki drill
and I'd jump down ready to help
with the plop-plop unwound satin twill,
and the cambrics, cashmeres and fine welts.

I'd jump down eager to help –
there were shelves of strong teak to the top –
to stack cambrics, cashmeres and bleached welts.
I remember your wholesaler's shop.

Victor

Today Mugabe's at the FAO in Rome. (An Ionesco farce?)
So many Shonas and Manicas are going hungry – one bowl of
    'sadza' a day.
We used to eat our fill even during WW2; no black child ever
    starved.

But you loved America – you'd drawl, 'This is mighty fine ranching
    country.'
Al Capone and his Chicago gangsters fascinated you – they'd
    emigrated from Italy
like you to Southern Rhodesia. 'O Italy, where are you now?'

It was in Chicago you died, suddenly in your bed, four squares
of chocolate eaten, the wrapping thrown aside, when Sylvia found
    you
smiling beatifically, after she'd done the dishes.

Mugabe's land was a fertile earth, now bruised and seared.
No medicines for the sick, for those with Aids. Your sickness
was for home; for that blond German boy at school with you in
    Lausanne.

He had no idea why you were leaving. I look at him now, front row
in your school photo . . . you were good at Latin, but they didn't do
much of that at Prince Edward's, sent you to cadet-camp instead.

Victor Ludorum, victorious, victory – no, these do not apply.
You'd ask me to tell Mum and Dad you'd die young, very young,
but they must not grieve, absolutely no grieving for a non-achiever.

Your forever hero, Napoleon Bonaparte – there's an achiever:
Austerlitz, Iéna, Friedland. And he'd remember his soldiers' ailments
from a previous battle: 'How's your toothache?' he'd enquire.

Robert Mugabe a hero? He's only achieved the ruin of Zimbabwe –
like those other ruins we'd visit, entering the Temple with hushed
    breath.
On a list of nations Zimbabwe comes last, even after Zambia.

Victor, you went from Italy to Africa. Mugabe and his henchmen
     went
from Africa to Rome, but Berlusconi didn't invite them to his
     banquet.
They ate in a *trattoria* in Trastevere – were offered doggy-bags to
     take home.

A POW to his Mother in Naples

Cara mammina,
Here I am – alive!
The desert's far behind us now.
They brought us south
to this British Colony
called Southern Rhodesia
after some big businessman.

I do miss the sea,
those sunsets on the Bay –
this country's landlocked.
We're all together: me, Gino, Guido and Alberto,
in a camp near a place called 'Gatooma',
about a kilometre from a GOLD MINE!
The wheel hums as I write.

The other day
I thought I saw a nugget
glinting in the sun. *Madonna Mia!*
What I couldn't buy you with one of those –
I'd love to see gold pins in your hair,
instead of those plain ones
you inherited from *la nonna*.

These English are 'decent chaps',
they let us do things to pass the time:
Guido and Alberto are making ice-cream again
and selling it in the town;
as for me, it's just sewing-boxes, wooden,
just like yours, with compartments
for the different coloured reels.

I wonder what you're all doing today
for *La Festa del Redentore*?
I'll be with you for the next one,
You'll see. Kiss everyone for me
and ask *il babbo* to keep my lathe well oiled.
Tuo figlio che t'ama tanto, Giorgio.

P.S. I shall ask the English if I can have a guitar.

Who's Buddy Holly?

I really don't know. But ask me
about Robert Murolo and I'll burst into song.
Shall I sing you *'Llultimi rrose'*? Or
'Quando shpunta la luna a marechiare,
pur li pisci ci fanno l'amore'?

And the songs of the Mussolini era
still send shivers down my spine –
like *'Giovinezza'*, the Fascist anthem
Toscanini refused to conduct at La Scala
and soon after left for the USA.

When they invaded Abyssinia you could hear
'Facietta Nera bell 'Abyssina, e per bandiera
ti darem la Italiana', on every street corner.
In the *trattorie* soldiers would sing: *'Quando saremo*
vicino a te, noi ti darem il nostro Duce e il nostro Re.'

Then in Paris, I remember *'Boum, pourquoi mon coeur*
fait boum' by Jean Sablon. And Trenet's *'La Mer'*,
with those silvery reflections dancing on it.
Also Edith Piaf's drifting dead leaves; her enthusiasm
for the colour pink, though her 'little dress' was always black.

Saturday

morning was piano-lesson day,
first at her flat, later
at the Rhodesian College of Music
which she founded – however
I preferred her flat,
less formal, more intimate . . .
though in her room at College
were two Bechstein grands,
so when I could tackle a concerto
she'd play the orchestral part
on the other. Our thoughts intertwined,
we were soul-mates in the 'Adagio'
of K. 488 in F sharp minor (divine key).
I loved her too when she'd drop
ash over my keyboard,
one eye shut against the smoke,
while suggesting some point of expression.

Then one day she went back to England
with her husband who'd been made Wing Commander.
I'd been betrayed; my exam marks fell.
She did write, however, aerogrammes from Bushey.

After the war she came back;
Saturday mornings again – Mozart.
I got 'Honours' for finals.

Chatting before the lesson
as we used to do, the subject
of the millions gassed in Auschwitz
came up; 'Good riddance,' she said,
'don't you agree?'

Rimini Beach

I learnt to walk
on the sand at Rimini,
my feet sunk into
those golden grains,
when I was nearly two
and my mother worried
I'd never learn,
never have the courage
to lift up one foot
after the other
without holding on
to someone or something.

I'm still holding on
if I possibly can –
and having to walk away
in childhood from everything
I'd learnt to love,
from '*la Giovanna*' (*gña-gña*),
from my room with the pink roses
from the marble-top table
to run around in the kitchen
and the long settee to play trains on –
to have to leave it all behind,
untaught me how to walk,
to lift each foot from the sand,
even now.

Two Musings on the City of Milan

1. Milan 1936

An open coach for the children in the park,
pulled by nanny-goats with sharpish horns.

A pond with rounded lips and paper boats
launched by little boys in sailor suits.

A vast cathedral: spiky Gothic spires,
the '*Madonnina*' looking like a doll.

And at the Station is a model ship,
the '*Rex*' you cannot pull my brother from –

I see his nose squashed flat upon the glass,
our parents shouting: 'It's now time to go.'

And layer-cakes for children in cafés
like '*Biffi*' and '*Savini*', where whipped cream

tops the tallest drinks, a spiral staircase
we'd try to dig beneath with long, long spoons.

And arias sung by mother in full flow
the morning after hearing them on stage.

Then just fog . . .

2. Milan 2006

Yes, do go back,
find the Central Station
(that monolith of Fascist architecture)
where you won't have arrived because you flew.

Then walk down Piazzale Fiume –
sorry, it's now called Piazza della Repubblica,
cross the tram-lines and you'll be standing
right in front of that apartment block.

Go in and talk to the *portinaia*
and tell her the exact lay-out of the rooms
in the flat on the seventh floor: how
the main lift came straight into the hall;

how the children's bathroom was of blue mosaics
and the parents' of pink marble; how the father
hailed Mussolini's motorcade with loud cheers
from the balcony with two fir-trees in large pots.

And the *portinaia* will say: '*Ma Signora!*
How do you remember all these details?
They're absolutely right, but the lady's out
so I cannot let you have the keys.'

And you'll walk away slowly,
whereas last time you'd packed fast
but left most things behind . . .

The Night of Broken Glass

Kristallnacht, 9 November 1938

The crystal shone
the shops grew dark
soon hope was gone
the faces stark.

The front door glass
was smashed to bits,
no one could pass
bonfires were lit.

Prayer-scrolls and books
blazed in the flames,
their owners shook
with fear and shame.

Synagogues burnt
razed to the ground,
the Holy Ark
smashed – for a lark.

Pastor von Jan
deplored that night
the ghoulish fun
but felt the might

of Nazi thugs
himself when they
left him for dead
beside a shed.

Stormtroopers stood
commanding Jews
to sweep the streets
in their bare feet.

*

November 10 . . .
The pale, cold sun
rose to a mass
of broken glass.

The Colossus

In July 1944, the Jews of Rhodes and Kos were packed into
three petrol-tankers and taken first to Piraeus, then to
Auschwitz. My grandfather and grandmother were among them.

You could have hung on to his leg,
his foot, or even just one toe;
but he'd turned himself away from you.
Anyway they'd packed you all down
in the bowels of three petrol-tankers.

You were too shocked, panicked, paralysed
to imagine him as you did in your youth
when you'd sail out between his giant legs –
their bronze sparkling in the Aegean sun –
to visit Kos or Karpathos or Khalke.

Then he would speak to you of strength,
of valorous deeds, of derring-do; now
you're caught like rats gnawing for food,
parched from lack of a single sip of water;
your imaginings deadened by terror.

And you prayed, 'Helios! Apollo! Sun-God!
Let us come back here to Rhodes
our island home these five hundred years.
The earthquake that destroyed you was nothing
compared with this man-made, man-planned Hell.'

My Grandmother

I'd love to see her again.
She was born on an Aegean island
surrounded by a turquoise, gentle,
rock-a-bye sea.

Home was in the harbour area –
always boats, some coming in, others leaving –
and the cries of fishermen,
the squish of fish in baskets,
the click of clogs on the pebbles.

That last time, three petrol-tankers
came to round her up,
to round them all up and take them
to a land-locked country
she'd hardly heard of,

with a language whose harsh syllables
rattled in her brain . . .
without the endless flow,
the mercy of the sea.

Grandfathers

He said his grandfather
should be exhumed. He'd been
a good man really, despite the chin.

I say my grandfather
should be exhumed. But first
he must be found; he too was a good man.

Somewhere between Pireaus and Poland
he'd been chucked out. You see
thirst had killed him on the train.

Fancy hanging him by a meat-hook,
the grandson said; and upside-down, his mistress
Clara Pettacci on another meat-hook beside him.

Fancy having to give him
his own urine to drink, I say.
I can hear his wife scream

as the guards prepare to throw
his body out of the heavy doors;
she pleads they throw her out too.

Day of Atonement

Tonight I see you, father,
in the reddish-blue suit you wore to synagogue,
your curly hair neatly restrained, black shoes
like mirrors; can smell the splash
of Eau-de-Cologne around your temples.

Mother, you're still busy in the kitchen
making sure the pot-roasted, honeyed chicken,
the golden rice, the salads and the soup
for breaking the twenty-four-hour fast
are all ready and dutifully waiting.

Then firmly you shut the kitchen door.
The house is stilled, becomes noiseless
with a solemn air, and it smells different.
We children go about quietly . . .
imbued with a new kind of respect.

In synagogue we're intoning 'Our Father, Our King',
that saddest of tunes in a minor key
with its load-bearing augmented seconds;
but we're joyful that last year at least
we were inscribed in the Book of Life.

When, after sunset, it's time to eat again,
we set off home with the customary headache.
We're invited to wash our hands and sit round the table.
Mother, you're disappointed that uncle must first
take a puff at his much-missed cigarette.

*

Now, all these years later
as we sing 'Avinu Malkeinu' with deeper voices,
I suddenly see the ones for whom
fasting was the order of the day, holding out
their soup cans with their skeletal arms.

Shoes

These are the children's shoes,
more pathetic, more troubling
than the grown-ups' ones.

I remember my cousin Rachelika
had a pair of lovely red ones
coveted by me whenever she wore them;

and her young twin sisters had pale blue ones
to match their coats – they must have been grimy
by the time they were pushed off the cattle truck.

Who are these women and men
sorting sandals, lace-ups, pumps,
character shoes from the feet of dead children?

When they go home, will they tell
their own children how their days were spent
building pyramids out of children's shoes?

No. 132540

Today I imagine a piece of bread
hot from the oven, with that smell
of pure white flour, unadulterated;
I taste the doughy middle, the crispy crust.

Not this rock-hard blackened end-of-loaf
I sometimes chip my teeth on,
with its acrid taste and greenish dough,
to go with our beetroot-peel soup.

I dream I'm home again, my wife and children
sitting round the table for the evening meal;
the cloth is white, the cutlery gleams.

Would I could plant one single poppy-seed
set on that plaited loaf into the heart
of these non-men to make them GOOD again.

Exorcism

for Miriam who made tapestries

Your tapestry, my dear,
of a street in Jerusalem
with its ancient arches
and minuscule windows
cut into the pink stone
talks to me of you.

(How long before these stones
are cleansed of blood?)

Outside streaky clouds
bless the pale-blue sky
that holds them, witness
to the shedding of blood.

The Chief Rabbi says
ethics must reinvent
the State of Israel,
and Israel must reinvent
what Jerusalem stands for.

TV lies twist their way to a hell
that is not Jerusalem,
not your ancient capital
which has long ago
washed the blood from its streets.

October

was the last time
we were together, both
looking out at the leaves
falling, falling
yellow, russet and brown
onto the paving-stones.

Your chair, as ever,
was by the window;
nor did you move it at night –
with the curtains half-drawn
you loved to contemplate the stars;
they spoke to you of the infinite.

I could see then
you were moving closer to death,
your great fatigue behind you;
and your frame becoming lighter,
more ready to be carried off, away
from all earthly things.

Empty Apartment

Then I shall close the door behind me
for the last time.

It will not be difficult –
I've practised that movement before.

The scent of her, her face-powder (Caron, always)
will have dispersed, mingled with the dust.

Furniture, carpets, pictures, bibelots, books
were packed up weeks ago.

There remain the walls that encased her,
that bounced her voice back like a soundboard;

the parquet floor too, a snaredrum
to her drum-stick footsteps.

And those large French windows –
her eyes passing through them longingly

to admire the three chestnut trees
that marked the seasons for her,

and sometimes brought her a stray bird
for long intimate conversations.

Yes, I shall know how to walk away
but not silently . . . not silently.

Apartment Block

It's still there;
straight and tall
dwarfing all
in the square.

Can't help but stare,
recall the fall
nothing could stall
of all that's dear.

Now years away
I see my room,
that second womb,
forced to betray.

But nothing's dead
lives in the head.

Astrakhan

The other day
I saw one
just like hers
on a blond girl
at the bank.

I noted how
the newborn lamb's
furry clusters
curled like ringlets
in a girl's hair.

As a child
I'd snuggle up
before she left
for La Scala
all dolled up.

When that life
brusquely ended
she stored the coat
with mothballs
in a trunk,

never to be
worn again
in the unsubtle,
crushing
African sun.

I heard once
these lambs are born
by the Volga
to the song
of the boatmen.

They say often
the ewe dies
while giving birth;
it is not
a lucky coat.

Regret

That day I gashed my father's palm
while he was driving me to school.
It bled. I grieved to do him harm.
My seat became a blood-filled pool
because I'd gashed my father's palm.
I'd said some nasty things; I was a fool
to gash my father's clean white palm
while he was driving me to school.

Tree

The tree in the garden
at the back of the house
had a branch coming out at right angles,
just perfect for hanging myself.

But the children shouted:
'A swing, a swing, Daddy,
can we have a swing?'
And he went to work making it.

He hadn't heard my silent cry –
not then, not ever.

In spring the tree bloomed.

Omega

I wish your heart was beating loudly still
Like this your Omega I've just rewound,
Its ticking hits a note that's sharp and shrill
As if to urge us on to life unbound.

Your life had been hard work and often fear
Of being forced away to unknown lands
Where some might mock your accent, often jeer
At all the dusty work of your clean hands.

It was your heart indeed that let you down,
Deciding to stop beating one cold night;
You lay stretched on your bed without a frown.
The rest of us were panicked, pale with fright.

I slid your gold-faced watch straight off your wrist.
It signals every day how much you're missed.

My Auntie Rica

She would get up and dance
with all of her body
clicking her fingers
stamping her feet
whenever that music
of the early pioneers
(chalutzim, kibbutzim)
filled up her dining-room,
the rhythm encircling
the table, the lamp,
the chairs, the sideboard,
and taking her by the waist
whirled her around
till tears wet her eyes
with longing to belong.

Annie B

So many times
I'd look at you
sitting in your wicker chair
on that porch in the clammy air,

and often think:
how can she sit and sit
and seem to read so little,
will she understand a jot or tittle?

Mechanically
you'd turn the page
as if that was the thing to do
so you'd deceive both us and you.

But thinking back,
now I'm your age,
I know that inner urge to stare
at things that are no longer there,

yet did exist
in early youth,
which we miss and mourn
and know cannot return.

My Piano Speaks

Where are you? Where have you gone?
It's been so long since I heard myself.
The room has gone unnervingly quiet.
I'm dying of silence. Occasionally,
when you brush a duster over my keys
I hear a distant *glissando* . . .
But I want true sounds again, even
those loud, assertive scales will do,
or the more intimate, sadder ones.

I miss your fingers touching me,
at times *con forza* at others *con amore*.
I want to tremble with my vibrating strings,
to hear the clamour of clashing chords,
to see the hammers do their vertical dance
and the dampers stay up a while longer
to give more resonance.

Come back now – it's been too long.
Start with a simple melody
from, say, Schumann's *'Kinderscenen'*,
pretend you're a child again,
take me back to childhood with you;
let's play his 'Rocking-Horse'
and the 'Child Falling Asleep'.

Take me back . . . [*ppp* and fading] . . . take me back

Mothers Can Get On Your Nerves

Mine told me
always to put a fresh dress on when visitors came to tea.
(Well, I didn't, but they still seemed to like me.)

Mine often said:
'*il faut souffrir pour être belle.*'
(But I didn't want to suffer, nor to be beautiful.)

Mine told me
to practise more scales and arpeggios.
(But I hated them, they had no tune.)

Mine told me
not to peer so closely at the book when doing my homework.
(Well, I needed to, and my eyes haven't gone squinty.)

Mine told me
to smile nicely when people talked to me.
(What, even if I thought they were awful?)

Mine ordered me
to curtsey to my uncle when saying goodnight.
(Who did he think he was, God Almighty?)

Mine pleaded with me
to stop behaving like a teenager.
(Well, I was a teenager, so what did she expect?)

I Find a Photo of Lydia, My Children's Nanny

Above the line of nappies smiles your face,
Its cheeks so round and black and shiny-clean;
To unpeg each white square you have to lean
And show your silk headscarf bordered with lace.
You tended my two girls with such fine grace
And they responded, always very keen
To play inside your 'Kaia' with its gleam
Of cleanliness and its uncluttered space.

But then one day I wanted you to read
To them, forgot you hadn't been to school,
Insisted on my children's urgent need
To know *Alice in Wonderland*. A fool
I was; sacked you on the spot. 'No bad deed,
Madam, father too poor to pay for school.'

Statue of Sigmund Freud Seated

Outside the Tavistock Centre, London NW3

He could be a rabbi – his father was –
but he's listening, not sermonising;
he wants to interpret and understand.
It helps him concentrate to fit his thumbs
into the pockets of his waistcoat.

There's a fob-chain hanging there too,
but the hour's consultation doesn't feature
in this timeless depiction of a searcher.
Stone rectangles form the folds of his trousers
that hang over his polished shoes.

Here in Hampstead he's an outsider –
in his bourgeois apartment at 19 Bergasse
he wasn't . . . until they came and ordered him out.
The couch, now exhibited in Maresfield Gardens,
is empty of the recliners' dreams and fantasies.

At the Flicks

Sir William Hamilton –
they call him 'Il Cavaliere' in Naples –
has just bid his butler straighten
his 'Great Masters'; doesn't he know
it's bad luck for pictures to hang askew?

Out of the tall windows
we see Vesuvius smoking, and on the horizon
Pompeii and Herculaneum; in the Bay
an elegant fleet of war vessels,
their flares flickering in the fading light.

Fast-forward – a full-figured girl (Vivien Leigh)
with auburn hair, violet eyes and ripe lips,
stands in the ornate drawing-room struggling
to read a letter from her sailor lover,
one Horatio Nelson (Laurence Olivier).

How handsome he'd looked despite his eye-patch!
How tightly he'd embraced her with just one arm!
We schoolgirls sitting in the Palace Theatre
in our 9d seats at the back shut our eyes
and dream of being kissed like that one day . . .

Now she's reading his letter aloud – tears fill her eyes:
'My dearest beloved Emma, the dear friend of my bosom,
the signal has been made that the enemy's combined fleet
are coming out of port. We have very little wind
so that I have no hopes of seeing them before tomorrow.'

The letter is dated October 19, 1805 aboard the *Victory*.
We've done that bit of history, we know what's going to happen.
When it continues: 'May the God of battles crown
my endeavours with success', we sob and cry out:
'No, don't do it! Please don't, you'll get killed.'

The Horses

'Waterloo! Waterloo! Waterloo! Morne plaine!'
'L'Expiation', Victor Hugo

We had not realised it was so near Brussels,
that bloody field where three armies clashed.
They'd raised a platform for visitors to get
a keener view of the dead in torn uniforms,
their epaulettes and medals half-buried in mud.

First we took a stroll to Wellington's HQ,
an old coaching inn where his horses were housed;
the equerries brushing their flanks till they shone,
combing their swish tails, whispering gently.
The Iron Duke's room was square and unfussy.

Then to the platform overlooking the battle:
poor horses, silently neighing in pain,
their nostrils inflated from the effort to breathe:
bodies still rearing from the terror of drums.
And flags in tatters, the rags of the battle.

Talking to My Teenage Pin-Up Boy

When I grew older
I went to look for you
at that house in Lerici;
but the Signora told me
you wouldn't be back till after dark –
you'd sailed off in your yacht, *Ariel*.

And many years later
I went to find you
in your college at Oxford
but you'd been sent down
for distributing your pamphlet
The Necessity of Atheism.

And years after still
I did find something of you
in the Bodleian: a piece of hair,
rich and curly, and the guitar
you gave to Jane at Casa Magni
telling her it had learned all the harmonies.

And I went to look
for the lovely Harriet, your sixteen-year-old
wife and soul-mate,
but alas she lay drowned
at the bottom of the Serpentine,
carrying (they said) another's child.

I looked for you too
in Skinner Street
where the Godwins lived,
but you'd eloped with Mary
and set sail for France, impatiently
hiring a boat of your own.

And I saw, like Trelawny,
your half-eaten body washed up
on the beach at Via Reggio,
a volume of Sophocles in one pocket
and Keats's poems in the other,
as if you were reading till the last moment.

But now, in my old age,
I find you most of all
in the breath of the Wild West Wind,
in the grace of Intellectual Beauty,
and in all things that are dearer for their mystery.
In that Spirit of Delight which is love and life.

And lucky girl, Emilia Viviani,
to be invited to sail away with you
to that island paradise full of books and music:
      'It is an isle under Ionian skies,
      beautiful as a wreck of Paradise.'

December at the Royal Free

Corridors are long;
heels stiletto up and down,
now louder, now softer,
click-clacking on the slippery lino.

Trolleys rattle, mops squidge,
jugs shake, water swishes.
Now it's midnight: pills swallowed,
lights out . . . NO, lights on and on . . .

Bleepers bleeping, pagers paging,
there's urgency in some,
others warn feebly as doors squeak;
the air-conditioning hums-ums-ums.

*

Outside through the grime
of sealed windows
London breathes regularly
but sleeps fitfully.

The green Holiday Inn sign
beckons me to my street,
to my green laurel hedge,
to greenness.

Meeting Point

I set off on a journey once,
and halfway there
I met myself returning.

I questioned her most vehemently,
how was it over there,
had it been worth the going?

She offered me no answer
but stared right down
at the spot where we were meeting.

And soon she disappeared
and I resumed my journey,
joyful at my ignorance.

Portrait of the Artist as an Old Woman

Two missing molars,
three incisors tastefully re-covered,
canines regally crowned
but gums still bleeding.

Tinted hair lies colourful
but occasional parting reveals white scalp.
Cataracts obfuscate visual reality
to create other-worldly (wordly?) images.

And bones . . . ah bones! Often creak/crack;
joints seize up in sudden cramp,
stiffen for no good reason.
Life becomes mechanical.

Fearfully, she descends the stairs
holding tight the handrail
in dread of tripping or losing strength,
or the unexpected dizzy spell.

Thankfully, the mind endures,
now well-stocked with useful/useless
information – facts still do confuse –
sometimes with true knowledge.

And there is the heart,
inured to shocks and pain
with a sturdy shield protecting it
which she'll sometimes slip off . . .

And see: a poem is written.

Dark Matter

What's important is
the poem not yet written,
embedded deep inside,
that on cheerless nights
threatens to surface
and so lose its mystery.

What counts is
the unformulated word
that hasn't yet got yoked to meaning
nor shackled itself
in the straitjacket
of exactitudes.

What echoes is
the word that's still pure sound
in no particular tonality,
without time-signature or bar-lines;
nor does it rest at a cadential point.
It has no beginning and no end . . .

What lives is
the uncreated; in the soil
of some anterior life –
timid, hidden, reluctant –
yet longing, oh so longing
to surface into sunlight.

Container

We're told that Tambimuttu,
long-time editor of *Poetry London*,
kept contributions to his magazine
in a chamber pot under his bed.

The metaphor is pleasing:
poems as the body's wreckage,
that which if held within
poisons the system.

An inability to write
is a form of constipation
which only a potent purge
(anger, grief) can unblock.

The opposite is logorrhea,
an uncontrollable flow
of yellow words that create
nausea and verbal sickness.

How like a cleansing bowel movement
is the issuing forth of a poem –
Tambi knew it well
and kept a suitable container.

No Ornithologist

I do not know the names of birds
But love their songs that have no words.

The flute-like ones both wild and shrill
That pierce the ear with a demon trill.

Like Messiaen I lie in wait
To tempt them with some wormy bait.

A melody first far then near . . .
How come it's turned into a jeer?

And others seem to quarrel like
A married couple bent on strife.

Now listen here's a sadder song
That comes in when the dusk is long,

And takes us to a view of death,
And sings us to our dying breath.

What Are Words For?

Polonius: 'What do you read, my Lord?'
Hamlet: 'Words, words, words.'

Words are for conveying meaning;
Words are for concealing it.

Words are for being polite;
Words are for being abusive.

Words are for painting pictures;
Words are for structuring gaps.

Words are for shouting cacophonies;
Words are for achieving silence.

Words serve to calculate immensity;
Words are for measuring the minuscule.

Words are for creating abstractions;
Words are for securing concreteness.

How can we write but with words?

Clouds

'Do you see yonder cloud that's almost in shape of a camel?'
(Hamlet)

Some are wisps of hair
up and up in the cold sky,
ready to turn to ice. Sailors
believed they brought windy weather.

Heavy with darkness
are the ones that press on the head,
down as far as they dare,
and burst into storm.

And there are rosy openings
for breathing between clouds –
we know they'll get thinner
and eventually disappear.

But on an aeroplane, sitting
above the clouds, how white and innocent
they look, soft as a pile of cushions
to fall into and cuddle.

Often I see faces in the clouds:
a Roman Emperor wearing his laurels,
or my father's stern and anxious,
and (disturbingly) my own.

Worms

King: 'Now, Hamlet, where's Polonius?'
Hamlet: 'At supper.'
King: 'At supper! Where?'
Hamlet: 'Not where he eats, but where he is eaten.'

Worms lie wriggling in the warmth
of the earth, near its hearth,
underbelly slithering along it.

My fleshy mouth
rounds its lips to make the name,
pulpous like their body.

I have only foot contact
with the sand – their whole length
brushes through it, feels each grain.

Limblessness keeps them
close to the earth – my limbs
distance me from it.

Loam, clay, mud are theirs,
ours in death alone – unless
we opt to be burnt to ash,

and deny the worms our flesh.

To a Twopenny Piece

Not for ever will you be as bright as now,
but spent and tarnished
and eventually withdrawn or buried.

A crowned queen whose time has come,
though rich in life and eternal
like this embossed flower.

Who knows how many hands
will have handled you, touched
and offered you to someone else

in search of durance.
Trust your body's circle,
here's no beginning and no end.

Folk Tale

In the ancient city of Kraków
lived a girl with gold-yellow hair
and blue eyes the colour of sapphires.

Sadly she was a princess
and Wanda her true Polish name,
which her father rendered 'Wandouchka'.

One day a German invader,
a prince from over the river,
saw her and straightaway loved her.

And swore to retreat to his country
if she'd go with him as his bride
to live over there far from Poland.

But she refused. Could not marry
an enemy prince, a German.
So she jumped into the Vistula.

It's said that on a hot summer's day
when the Vistula's water is clear
a girl's hair is seen floating there.

Disillusion

Penelope weaves and weaves,
Still in her prime,
To hasten time
Until Odysseus leaves
That enchantress Calypso.
But she's forgetting his face,
His touch, his grace,
That glance of the hero.

And the suitors fail to please:
One's hirsute, has halitosis,
Another drinks to ease neurosis,
Yet another reeks of cheese.

Then, one ordinary lonely night,
Comes her love, old, gaunt, and slight.

Beauty and the Beast

As Belle grew up surrounded by her books
She learned to scorn broad chests, biceps, good looks,
In favour of a quality of mind,
Sensitivity, a heart that's kind.

She got her wish. The Beast was gruff but bright,
Considerate, aware, and did not slight
Her playing seated at the virginal.
This Beast, she soon resolved, would have her all.

Now what was her dismay when at the feast
To mark the transformation of the Beast
There stepped out of the sweaty pelt a youth
As bland as all the rest, sleek-haired and couth.

So don't believe the 'ever after' bit
For Belle beheld the schmaltzy Prince, and quit.

A Christmas Poem

Mother Christmas sulked –
She had reason to –
Hubby wouldn't let her have a turn
At taking kids their due.

'You haven't got a licence.
A sleigh is not a car.
You need a special flair
To drive it fast and far.

And what is more, my dear,
A reindeer's not a dog.
It needs some expert handling
To drive it through the fog.

Anyway you're much too fat,
And chimneys can be hot.
I fear you may be stuck in there
And badly burn your bot.'

So poor old Mother Christmas
Didn't have a chance;
She'd have to wait a hundred years
For men to change their stance.

But Lapland was ahead of things:
One day a feisty girl
Jumped on a reindeered sleigh,
Tossed a blond curl

And away, away, away . . .

Love Sonnet for the Twenty-First Century

If YouTube
And iPod
And YouBoob
While I nod,

And you Twitter
And I Google
And we flitter
To find Froogle;

You'll be he-mail
And you'll blog,
I'll be fe-mail
And I'll snog.

Then we'll bling
and swing and sing.